TIME

By Alan Watts
Book VI in the Illustrated Series
THE ESSENCE OF ALAN WATTS

ALAN WATTS " . . . has provided a series
of sensitively illustrated jewel-books for
the searching spirits of this century . . . . "
—Joseph Campbell

Photographs by Joseph McHugh

CELESTIAL ARTS
Millbrae, California

First Printing, January 1975
Made in the United States of America
Cover photo of Alan Watts by Margo Moore

Library of Congress Cataloging in Publication Data

Watts, Alan Wilson, 1915-1973
   Time.

   (His The essence of Alan Watts ; book 6)
   1. Time. I. Title.
B945.W321 1974, vol. 6 (BD638) 191s (115) 74-25826
ISBN 0-912310-86-3

THE STORY OF ALAN WATTS

For more than twenty years Alan Watts earned a reputation as the foremost interpreter of Eastern philosophies to the West. Beginning at the age of 20, when he wrote *The Spirit of Zen*, he developed an audience of millions who were enriched by his offerings through books, tape recordings, radio, television, and public lectures.

He wrote 25 books, each building toward a personal philosophy that he shared, in complete candor and joy, with his readers and listeners throughout the world. They presented a model of individuality and self-expression that can be matched by few contemporaries. His life and work reflect an astonishing adventure: he was editor, Anglican priest, graduate dean, broadcaster, and author-lecturer. He had fascinations for cooking, calligraphy, singing, and dancing. He held fellowships from Harvard University and the Bollingen Foundation and was Episcopal Chaplain at Northwestern University. He became professor and dean of the American Academy of Asian Studies in San Francisco, made the television series "Eastern Wisdom and Modern Life" for the National Educational Television, and served as visiting consultant to many psychiatric institutes and hospitals. He traveled widely with students in Japan.

Born in England in 1915, Alan Watts attended King's School Canterbury, served on the Council of the World Congress of Faiths (1936–38), and came to the United States in 1938. He held a Master's Degree in Theology from Seabury-Western Theological Seminary and an Honorary D.D. from the University of Vermont in recognition of his work in Comparative Religion.

Alan Watts died in 1973. *The Essence of Alan Watts*, a series of nine books in the unique *Celestial Arts* format, includes edited transcripts by his wife, Mary Jane Watts, of videotaped lectures that were produced by his friend, Henry Jacobs, and filmed by his son, Mark Watts, in the last years of his life.

Time. What is time?

St. Augustine of Hippo when asked, "What is time?" said, "I know what it is, but when you ask me I don't." Yet it is absolutely fundamental to our life: "Time is money." "I don't have enough time." "Time flies." "Time drags."

I think we should question what time is, because of our ordinary common sense we think of it as a one-way motion from the past through the present and on into the future. That carries with it the impression that life moves from the past to the future in such a way that what happens now and what will happen is always the result of what has happened in the past. In other words, we seem to be driven along.

Once it was fashionable in psychology for people to speak of man's instincts, the instinct for survival, an instinct to make love, and so on. But nowadays that word has become unfashionable and psychologists tend instead to use the word *drive*, and to speak of the need for food as a drive, the need for survival or for sex as drives. That's a very significant word because it's brought out by people who feel driven. Personally, if I feel hungry I don't feel driven; if I feel lusty I don't feel driven; I don't say, "Oh, excuse me but I have to eat," or, "Excuse me but I need to fulfill my sexual urges." I say, "Hooray!" I identify myself with my drives. They are me, and I don't take a passive attitude towards them and apologize for them. So the whole idea of our being driven is connected with the idea of causality, of life moving under the power of the past. That is so ingrained in our common sense that it's very difficult to get rid of it. But I want to turn it round completely and say the past is the result of the present.

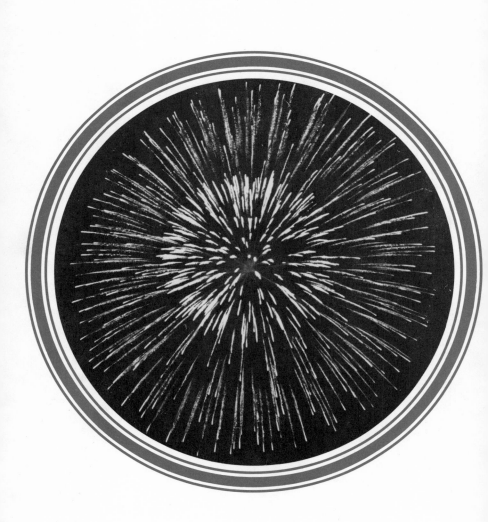

From one point of view that is very obvious. For example, let us suppose that this universe started with a big bang as some cosmologists believe. Now when that bang happened, it was the present, wasn't it? And so the universe began in what we will call a *now* moment, then it goes on doing its stuff. When any event that we now call past came into being, it came into being in the present and out of the present. That's one way of seeing it.

But before we get further involved in this, I want to draw your attention to a fallacy in the very commonsense idea of causality—events are caused by previous events from which they flow or necessarily result. To understand the fallacy of that idea, we have to begin by asking, "What do you mean by an event?" Let's take the event of a human being coming into the world. Now when does that event begin? Does it occur at the moment of parturition when the baby actually comes out of its mother? Or does the baby begin at the moment of conception? Or does a baby begin when it is a gleam in its father's eye? Or does a baby begin when the spermatozoa are generated in the father or the ova in the mother? Or could you say a baby begins when its father is born or when its mother is born? All these things can be thought of as beginnings, but we decide for purposes of legal registration that a life begins at the moment of parturition. And that is a purely arbitrary decision; it has validity only because we all agree about it.

Let me show you the same phenomenon in the dimension of space instead of the dimension of time. Let's ask, "How big is the sun?" Are we going to define the sun as limited by the extent of its fire? That's one possible definition. But we could equally well define the sphere of the sun by the extent of its light. And each of these would be reasonable choices. We have arbitrarily agreed to define the sun by the limit of its visible fire. But you see in these analogies that how big a thing is or how long an event is, is simply a matter of definition.

Therefore, when by the simple definition for purposes of discussion we have divided events into certain periods—the First World War began in 1914 and it ended in 1918 (actually, all those things which led up to the First World War started long before 1914, and the repercussions of that war continued long after 1918)—we sort of forget we do it. We have a puzzle, "How do events lead to each other?"

In reality there are no separate events. Life moves along like water, it's all connected as the source of the river is connected to the mouth and the ocean. All the events or things going on are like whirlpools in a stream. Today you see a whirlpool and tomorrow you see a whirlpool in the same place, but it isn't the same whirlpool because the water is changing every second.

What is happening is not really what we should call a whirlpool, but rather a whirlpooling. It is an *activity*, not a *thing*. And indeed every so-called thing can be called an event. We can call a house, *housing*, a mat, *matting*, and we could equally call a cat, a *catting*. So we could say, "The *catting* sat on the *matting*." And we would thereby have a world in which there were no things but only events. To give another illustration: A flame is something we say, "There is a flame on the candle." But it would be more correct to say, "There is a flaming on the candle," because a flame is a stream of hot gas.

Let's take another amusing example. *Fist* is a noun and fist looks like a thing, but what happens to the fist when I open my hand. I was fisting, now I'm handing, handing it to you. So every kind of so-called thing can be spoken of as an event and because events flow into each other, the fisting flows into the handing, we cannot say exactly where one ends and the other begins.

So, therefore, we do not need the idea of causality to explain how a prior event influences a following event. Consider it this way: Suppose I'm looking through a narrow slit in a fence, and a snake goes by. I've never seen a snake before, so it is mysterious. Through the fence I see first the snake's head, then I see a long trailing body, and then finally the tail. Then the snake turns around and goes back. Then I see first the head, and then after an interval the tail. Now if I call the head one event and the tail another, it will seem to me that the event *head* is the cause of the event *tail*. And the tail is the effect. But if I look at the whole snake I will see a head-tail snake and it would be simply absurd to say that the head of the snake is the cause of the tail, as if the snake came into being as a head first and then a tail. The snake comes into being out of its egg as a head-tail snake. And in exactly the same way all events are really one event. We are looking, when we talk about different events, at different sections or parts of one continuous happening.

Therefore, the idea of separate events, which have to be linked by a mysterious process called cause and effect, is completely unnecessary. But having thought that way, we think of present events as being caused by past events, and tend to regard ourselves as the *puppets* of the past, driven along by something that is always behind us.

It's very simple to overcome this impression. You begin with an experiment in meditation—approach the world through your ears. If you shut your eyes and make contact with reality purely with your ears, you will realize that the sounds you are hearing are all coming out of silence. It's curious isn't it because you hear all the realities, the sounds suddenly coming out of nothing. You don't see any reason for them to begin, they just appear and then they echo away through the corridors of the mind which we call memory.

Now if you open your eyes, it's a little harder to see this because unlike sound, the eyes sound static or rather, they see static. Everything looks still to your eyes, but you must understand that the world you are looking at is vibrating. All material things are vibrating and they are vibrating at you now in the same way as the sound was vibrating on your ears. In other words, the present world that you see is a vibration coming out of space just as the sound comes out of silence. It is coming out of nothing straight at you and echoing away into the past.

So the course of time is really very much like the course of a ship in the ocean. The ship leaves a wake behind it, and the wake fades out and tells us where the ship has been in just the same way as the past and our memory of the past tells us what we have done. But as we go back into the past, and we go back and back to prehistory and we use all kinds of instruments and scientific methods for detecting what happened, we eventually reach a point where all record of the past fades away in just the same way as the wake of a ship.

Now the important thing to remember in this illustration is that the wake doesn't drive the ship anymore than the tail wags the dog. The power, the source of the wake, is always in the ship itself which represents the present. You can't insist that the wake drives the ship. You can plot the course of the ship on graph paper and calculate a trend by seeing over what number of squares the ship has been doing its wiggling, and make predictions as to where it will go next. This would give you a trend as to where the ship is going and you might say, "Because we can plot the trend from the pattern which the ship has followed, we can tell where it is going and, therefore, we are inclined to think that where it has been will determine where it will go." But that is not actually the case. Where it has been is determined not by where it will go but where it is going. To put that more accurately, where it has been does not determine where it is going; where it is going determines where it has been.

If you insist that your present is the result of your past, you are like a person driving your car looking always in the rear-view mirror. You are not, as it were, open to the future, you are always looking back over your shoulder to find out what you ought to do. And this is something absolutely characteristic of us and this is why human beings find it difficult to learn and difficult to adapt themselves to new situations. Because we are always looking for precedents, for authority from the past for what we are supposed to do now, that gives us the impression the past is all-important and is the determinative factor in our behavior.

It isn't anything of the kind. The life, the creation, comes out of you now. In other words, don't look for the creation back here at the beginning of where the wake fades out. Don't look for the creation of the universe at some very far-distant point in time behind us. The creation of the universe is now in this present instant. This is where it all begins! And it trails away from here and eventually vanishes.

Now of course we have a method of passing the buck in all matters of responsibility by saying, "Well, the past is responsible for me." For instance, when dealing with a difficult child, we are apt to say, "Well, bang him about, beat him up, and maybe he'll change." But then we say, "No, that's not fair to the child to beat him up, because it was his parents' fault; they didn't bring him up properly." And so then we say, "Well, punish the parents." But the parents say, "Well, excuse me, but our parents were neurotic, too, and they brought us up badly so we couldn't help what we did." And since the grandparents are dead we can't get at them, and if we could we would pass the whole blame back to Adam and Eve. We would say, "They started all this mess." But then Eve would say, "No, the serpent tempted me and I did eat." Then it was the serpent's fault!

When God asked Eve, "Didst thou eat the fruit of the tree whereof I told thee thou shouldst not eat?" she said, "Oh, but the serpent tempted me and I did eat." And God looked at the serpent, and the serpent didn't make any excuse. He probably winked—because the serpent, being an angel, was wise enough to know where the present begins.

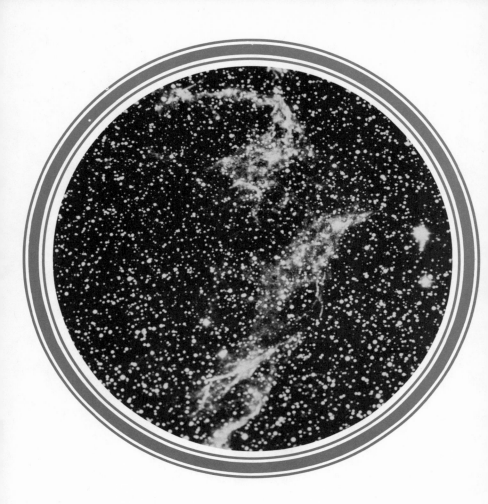

So you see, if you insist on being moved, being determined by the past, that's your game. But the fact of the matter is *it all starts right now.* But we like to establish a connectivity with the past because that gives other people the impression that we're sane. People ask, for example, why you do something. Now that's a ridiculous question. A child finds out that to irritate its parents it can always put the word *why* after any answer to a question. "Why does the sun shine?" and he gets an astronomical explanation, "Well, why does nuclear heat generate in star bodies?" "Oh, because it reaches a critical mass." "Well, why does it reach a critical mass?" And you can go on and on and on asking why until papa says, "Oh, shut up and suck your lollipop."

The question "why," because it can be asked interminably, never leads to any interesting answers. If you ask me then *why* am I proposing this, I could say, "Well, I'm making a living this way, or I have a message I want to get across to you." But that's not the reason. I am talking for the same reason that birds sing and the stars shine. I dig it. Why do I dig it? I could go on answering all sorts of questions about human motivation and psychology, but they wouldn't explain a thing, because explaining things by the past is really a refusal to explain them at all. All you're doing is postponing the explanation. You're putting it back and back and back and that explains nothing.

What does explain things is the present. Why do you do it now? Now this is a slight cheat because that doesn't explain it either, because what happens now, just as the sound comes out of silence, all this comes out of nowhere. All life suddenly emerges out of space—Bang! Right now!

And to ask again why does it happen is an unprofitable question because the interesting thing is not why but what. What happens? Not, why does it happen? I can say, "Well, I am doing this now because I did that then," and so I am producing for you a continuous line of thought, but actually I am doing it backwards. I'm doing it always from now and connecting up what I do now with what I did so that you can see a consistent story.

Now another interesting thing about this is that I can show you how the present changes the past. Let's take for example the order of words. Now words are strung out in a line just like we think events in time are strung out in a line and I can change a past word by a future word. If I say (taking a line from the poet Thomas Hood), "They went and told the sexton, and the sexton tolled the bell." You don't know what the first *told* means until you get the sexton; you don't know what the second *tolled* means until you get to the word *bell*. And so the later event changes the meaning of the former. Or you can say for example, "The bark of the tree," and the word *bark* has a certain meaning. Then I say, "The bark of the dog," and the later word has changed the meaning of the former one.

And so, in this way, when we write history we find that writing history is really an art. The historian keeps putting a fresh interpretation on past events and in that sense he is changing it. He is changing their meaning just like we were changing the meaning of a former word by a later word by saying, "They went and told the sexton and the sexton tolled the bell."

In this way you can experience a curious liberation from what the Hindus and the Buddhists call *karma*. The word *karma* in Sanskrit actually means doing, action. *Karma* comes from the root *kri* which simply means *to do*. When something happens to me, an accident or an illness, a Buddhist or a Hindu will say, "Well, it was your karma." In other words, you had done something in the past and you reap the unfortunate consequence in a later time. Now that's not the real meaning of karma. Karma does not mean cause and effect. It simply means doing. In other words, you are doing what is happening to you. And that, of course, depends upon how you define the word *you*. For example, consider breathing; am I doing it or is it happening to me? I am growing my hair; am I doing it or is it happening to me? You can look at it either way. I am being sick, or I am being destroyed in an accident—if I define myself as the whole field of events, the organism-environment field which is the real me, then all the things that happen to me may be called my doing. And that is the real sense of karma.

But when we speak about freedom from karma, freedom from being the puppet of the past, that simply involves a change in our thinking. It involves getting rid of the habit of thought whereby we define ourselves as the result of what has gone before. We instead get into the more plausible, more reasonable habit of thought in which we don't define ourselves in terms of what we've done before but in terms of what we're doing now. And that is liberation from the ridiculous situation of being a dog wagged by its tail.